"Dedicated to all the brave single women still trying to find love in a dating world that makes no sense."

I'm the Ghost of Gold Digger Pride,

From the era of pearls, respect
— and a strong man by your side.

Back in my day,
men were proud to take you out,

They dressed sharp, brought flowers,
tried hard to stand out.

Now men cry "gold digger" —
it's the new beta broke boy sting,

They want sex and attention
without offering a thing.

Got called a gold digger — by a man with no flair?
Don't get rattled — just pull up a chair.

It's not you, it's him — that much is clear.
Let's go through the reasons he smeared you, dear.

He called you a gold digger?

That's just code,

For "she won't help me carry
my financial load."

He called you a gold digger

Because he wants the beauty,
grace — not the spend!

The look of a Barbie with the cost
of a friend.

He called you a gold digger

Because he paid for your meal
and didn't get sex,

So clearly, your standards must
be complex.

He called you a gold digger

Because he can't afford you —
but wants a top-tier pearl!

He doesn't want to date
his budget type of girl.

He called you a gold digger

Because he's a pussy man, a beta male,

He wants convenience, free, or everything on sale.

He called you a gold digger

Because he thinks if he pays, he's being played!

But your time, your effort, and sex? Fair trade!

He called you a gold digger

Because Tammy used him
10 years ago,

Now women must split or pay
and be good to go!

He called you a gold digger

Because he knows he can't provide!

So he labels you first — to save his pride.

He called you a gold digger

Because your shine made him feel like less,

So he blamed your standards — instead of his mess.

He called you a gold digger

Because he wants thin and pretty,
but also you to pay,

He's not a masculine man — he's
just closeted gay.

He called you a gold digger

Because he knows he's not a high-value guy,

The thought of Andrew Tate makes him cry.

He called you a gold digger

Because he gave no effort, no time, no clue,

But swore he was "a prize" — and you should pursue.

He called you a gold digger

Because you had standards built for a man — not a boy,

You deserve love, provision, and eternal joy.

He called you a gold digger

Because he realized he'd need to grow and succeed —

And he's not what a classy, successful girl needs.

He called you a gold digger

Because you have what he can't obtain,

So he blamed your standards —
to ease his shame.

He called you a gold digger

Because he gives nothing and
calls you crazy,

It's just to cover he's broke,
unmotivated, and lazy.

He called you a gold digger

Because he can't afford you,
but still made the try,

Then called you a gold digger —
cheap man's cry.

Gold Diggers Through the Ages
Specimen:
The Blame-Shifter
Accuses Women When Rejected

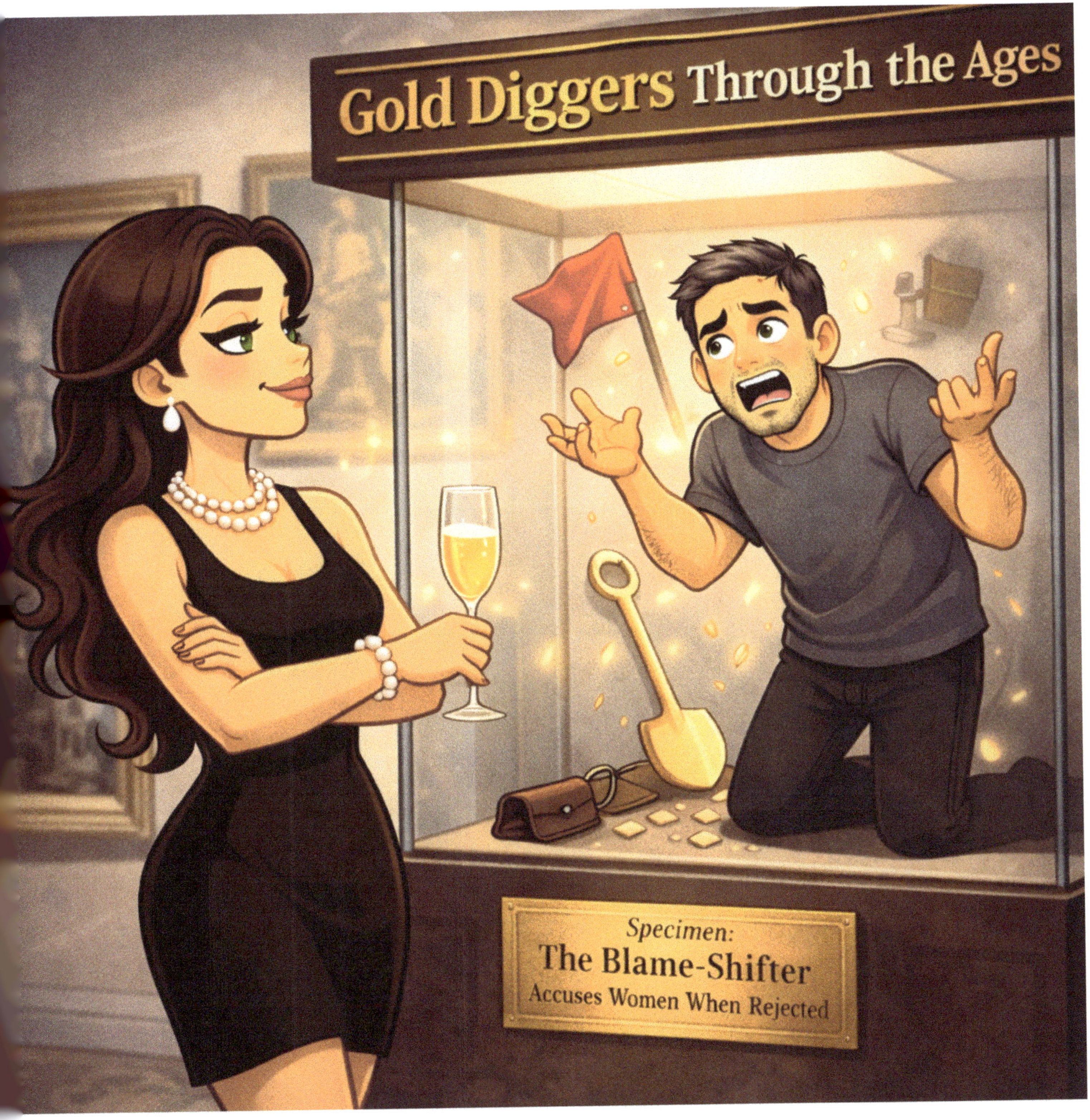

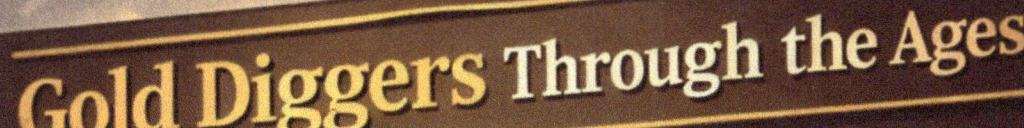

He called you a gold digger

Because you asked for more than a casual "thing,"

He wanted wife perks — with no wedding ring.

He called you a gold digger

Because he gives nothing and calls you unstable,

To cover he's lazy and financially unable.

He called you a gold digger?
Good — you passed the test,
That means your standards
scared off the little pest.

Don't get quiet — don't shrink —
don't sway,
Here's how to clap back, the old-
school way.

Be Direct

You called me a gold digger —
how telling, how small,
A successful man wouldn't go
there at all!

I just wasn't feeling the
chemistry,
But you're broke — so you
blamed lack of financial
supremacy.

Teach Him

You wanted my time,
my looks, and more,
Didn't want to pay for dinner —
and still tried to score.

A real man courts, is kind, and
true —
You're just a little boy... so f* to
the you.

Be Honest

If I was a gold digger,
I wouldn't have gone on the date,
I saw the Civic — and the two
roommates.

So saying that word just let me
see,
This is about you — not me.

Congratulations!

You got called a gold digger by a boy,

Who sang the poor man's anthem:
"She's a gold digger!"
with joy.

Thirsty girls fold, shrink down,
or even pay —

But you, smart flower,
are too high-value to play.